― MADE EASY PRESS ―

2024 • 2025
Christian
Monthly Planner

Two-Year Schedule Organizer with Holidays, Reflections, and Inspiring Bible Verses and Scripture for Women to Keep Track of Your Appointments, Goals, and Activities

 Producer & International Distributor
eBookPro Publishing
www.ebook-pro.com

2024-2025 Christian Monthly Planner:

Two-Year Schedule Organizer with Holidays, Reflections, and Inspiring Bible Verses and Scripture for Women to Keep Track of Your Appointments, Goals, and Activities

Made Easy Press

Copyright © 2023 Made Easy Press

All rights reserved; No parts of this book may be reproduced or transmitted in any form or by any means, electronic or mechanical, including photocopying, recording, taping, or by any information retrieval system, without the permission, in writing, of the author.

Contact: agency@ebook-pro.com
ISBN 9789655753929

2024

January

su	mo	tu	we	th	fr	sa
	1	2	3	4	5	6
7	8	9	10	11	12	13
14	15	16	17	18	19	20
21	22	23	24	25	26	27
28	29	30	31			

February

su	mo	tu	we	th	fr	sa
				1	2	3
4	5	6	7	8	9	10
11	12	13	14	15	16	17
18	19	20	21	22	23	24
25	26	27	28	29		

March

su	mo	tu	we	th	fr	sa
					1	2
3	4	5	6	7	8	9
10	11	12	13	14	15	16
17	18	19	20	21	22	23
24	25	26	27	28	29	30
31						

April

su	mo	tu	we	th	fr	sa
	1	2	3	4	5	6
7	8	9	10	11	12	13
14	15	16	17	18	19	20
21	22	23	24	25	26	27
28	29	30				

May

su	mo	tu	we	th	fr	sa
			1	2	3	4
5	6	7	8	9	10	11
12	13	14	15	16	17	18
19	20	21	22	23	24	25
26	27	28	29	30	31	

June

su	mo	tu	we	th	fr	sa
						1
2	3	4	5	6	7	8
9	10	11	12	13	14	15
16	17	18	19	20	21	22
23	24	25	26	27	28	29
30						

July

su	mo	tu	we	th	fr	sa
	1	2	3	4	5	6
7	8	9	10	11	12	13
14	15	16	17	18	19	20
21	22	23	24	25	26	27
28	29	30	31			

August

su	mo	tu	we	th	fr	sa
				1	2	3
4	5	6	7	8	9	10
11	12	13	14	15	16	17
18	19	20	21	22	23	24
25	26	27	28	29	30	31

September

su	mo	tu	we	th	fr	sa
1	2	3	4	5	6	7
8	9	10	11	12	13	14
15	16	17	18	19	20	21
22	23	24	25	26	27	28
29	30					

October

su	mo	tu	we	th	fr	sa
		1	2	3	4	5
6	7	8	9	10	11	12
13	14	15	16	17	18	19
20	21	22	23	24	25	26
27	28	29	30	31		

November

su	mo	tu	we	th	fr	sa
					1	2
3	4	5	6	7	8	9
10	11	12	13	14	15	16
17	18	19	20	21	22	23
24	25	26	27	28	29	30

December

su	mo	tu	we	th	fr	sa
1	2	3	4	5	6	7
8	9	10	11	12	13	14
15	16	17	18	19	20	21
22	23	24	25	26	27	28
29	30	31				

2025

January

su	mo	tu	we	th	fr	sa
			1	2	3	4
5	6	7	8	9	10	11
12	13	14	15	16	17	18
19	20	21	22	23	24	25
26	27	28	29	30	31	

February

su	mo	tu	we	th	fr	sa
						1
2	3	4	5	6	7	8
9	10	11	12	13	14	15
16	17	18	19	20	21	22
23	24	25	26	27	28	

March

su	mo	tu	we	th	fr	sa
						1
2	3	4	5	6	7	8
9	10	11	12	13	14	15
16	17	18	19	20	21	22
23	24	25	26	27	28	29
30	31					

April

su	mo	tu	we	th	fr	sa
		1	2	3	4	5
6	7	8	9	10	11	12
13	14	15	16	17	18	19
20	21	22	23	24	25	26
27	28	29	30			

May

su	mo	tu	we	th	fr	sa
				1	2	3
4	5	6	7	8	9	10
11	12	13	14	15	16	17
18	19	20	21	22	23	24
25	26	27	28	29	30	31

June

su	mo	tu	we	th	fr	sa
1	2	3	4	5	6	7
8	9	10	11	12	13	14
15	16	17	18	19	20	21
22	23	24	25	26	27	28
29	30					

July

su	mo	tu	we	th	fr	sa
		1	2	3	4	5
6	7	8	9	10	11	12
13	14	15	16	17	18	19
20	21	22	23	24	25	26
27	28	29	30	31		

August

su	mo	tu	we	th	fr	sa
					1	2
3	4	5	6	7	8	9
10	11	12	13	14	15	16
17	18	19	20	21	22	23
24	25	26	27	28	29	30
31						

September

su	mo	tu	we	th	fr	sa
	1	2	3	4	5	6
7	8	9	10	11	12	13
14	15	16	17	18	19	20
21	22	23	24	25	26	27
28	29	30				

October

su	mo	tu	we	th	fr	sa
			1	2	3	4
5	6	7	8	9	10	11
12	13	14	15	16	17	18
19	20	21	22	23	24	25
26	27	28	29	30	31	

November

su	mo	tu	we	th	fr	sa
						1
2	3	4	5	6	7	8
9	10	11	12	13	14	15
16	17	18	19	20	21	22
23	24	25	26	27	28	29
30						

December

su	mo	tu	we	th	fr	sa
	1	2	3	4	5	6
7	8	9	10	11	12	13
14	15	16	17	18	19	20
21	22	23	24	25	26	27
28	29	30	31			

Birthday Log

January

February

March

April

May

June

Birthday Log

July

August

September

October

November

December

My 2024 Resolutions

1.
2.
3.
4.
5.
6.
7.
8.
9.
10.
11.
12.
13.
14.
15.
16.
17.
18.

'For I know the plans I have for you,' declares the Lord, 'plans to prosper you and not to harm you, plans to give you hope and a future.'

– Jeremiah 29:11

January

I am the light of the world. Whoever follows me will never walk in darkness, but will have the light of life. John 8:12

monday	tuesday	wednesday	thursday
1 New Year's Day	2	3	4
8	9	10	11
15 Martin Luther King Day	16	17	18
22	23	24	25
29	30	31	

2024

Deuteronomy 31:6

*It is the Lord your God who goes with you.
He will not leave you or forsake you.*

friday	saturday	sunday
5	6	7
12	13	14
19	20	21
26	27	28

January

*The Lord is a refuge for the oppressed,
a stronghold in times of trouble.*

Psalm 9:9

Notes

*The Lord your God is with you,
the Mighty Warrior who saves.*

Zephaniah 3:17

Reflections

February

Whoever lives in love lives in God, and God in them.

1 John 4:16

monday	tuesday	wednesday	thursday
			1
5	6	7	8
12	13 Mardi Gras	14 Valentine's Day	15
19 Presidents Day	20	21	22
26	27	28	29

2024

The Lord is the everlasting God, the Creator of the ends of the earth.

Isaiah 40:28

friday	saturday	sunday
2 Groundhog Day	3	4
9	10	11
16	17	18
23	24	25

February

Always give yourselves fully to the work of the Lord, because you know that your labor in the Lord is not in vain.

1 Corinthians 15:58

Notes

For I know the plans I have for you, declares the Lord, plans to prosper you and not to harm you, plans to give you hope and a future.

Jeremiah 29:11

Reflections

March

For God so loved the world that he gave his one and only Son.   John 3:16

monday	tuesday	wednesday	thursday
4	5	6	7
11	12	13	14
Ramadan			
18	19	20	21
25	26	27	28

2024

Matthew 6:33 — *But seek first his kingdom and his righteousness, and all these things will be given to you as well.*

friday	saturday	sunday
1	2	3
8	9	10 Daylight Saving Starts
15	16	17 St. Patrick's Day
22	23	24 Purim
29 Good Friday	30	31 Easter

March

Trust in the Lord with all your heart, and do not lean on your own understanding.

Proverbs 3:5

Notes

I sought the Lord, and He heard me, And delivered me from all my fears.

Psalm 34:4

Reflections

April

When anxiety was great within me, your consolation brought me joy.   Psalm 94:19

monday	tuesday	wednesday	thursday
1 April Fool's Day	2	3	4
8	9	10 Eid al-Fitr	11
15	16	17	18
22 Earth Day	23 Passover	24	25
29	30		

2024

2 Corinthians 1:4

He comforts us in all our troubles, so that we can comfort those in any trouble with the comfort we ourselves receive from God.

friday	saturday	sunday
5	6	7
12	13	14
19	20	21
26	27	28

April

When you pass through the waters, I will be with you.

Isaiah 43:2

Notes

There is no fear in love.

1 John 4:18

Reflections

May

When perfection comes, the imperfect disappears.

1 Corinthians 13:10

monday	tuesday	wednesday	thursday
		1	2
6	7	8	9
13	14	15	16
20	21	22	23
27 Memorial Day	28	29	30

2024

May he give you the desire of your heart and make all your plans succeed.
Psalm 20:4

friday	saturday	sunday
3	4	5 Cinco de Mayo
10	11	12 Mother's Day
17	18 Armed Forces Day	19 Pentecost
24	25	26
31		

May

I will see the goodness of the Lord in the land of the living.

Psalm 27:13

Notes

A good name is more desirable than great riches.

Proverbs 22:1

Reflections

June

With man this is impossible, but not with God; all things are possible with God. — Mark 10:27

monday	tuesday	wednesday	thursday
3	4	5	6
10	11	12 *Shavuot*	13
17	18	19	20
24 *Eid al-Adha*	25	26	27

James 1:5

If any of you lacks wisdom, you should ask God, who gives generously to all without finding fault.

2024

friday	saturday	sunday
	1	2
7	8	9
14	15	16
Flag Day		Father's Day
21	22	23
28	29	30

June

*The wicked flee though no one pursues,
but the righteous are as bold as a lion.*

Proverbs 28:1

Notes

Very truly I tell you, the one who believes has eternal life.

John 6:47

Reflections

July

And do not forget to do good and to share with others, for with such sacrifices God is pleased. — *Hebrews 13:16*

monday	tuesday	wednesday	thursday
1	2	3	4 Independence Day
8 Muharram	9	10	11
15	16	17	18
22	23	24	25
29	30	31	

Our light and momentary troubles are achieving
2 Corinthians 4:17   for us an eternal glory that far outweighs them all.

friday	saturday	sunday
5	6	7
12	13	14 Bastille Day
19	20	21
26	27	28 Parents' Day

2024

July

Whatever happens, conduct yourselves in a manner worthy of the gospel of Christ.

Philippians 1:27

Notes

2024

*Through the endurance taught in the Scriptures and
the encouragement they provide we might have hope.*

Romans 15:4

Reflections

August

I keep my eyes always on the Lord; with him at my right hand, I will not be shaken. — Psalm 16:8

monday	tuesday	wednesday	thursday
			1
5	6	7	8
12	13	14	15
19	20	21	22
26	27	28	29

2024

Let us not become weary in doing good.
Galatians 6:9

friday	saturday	sunday	
2	3	4	
9	10	11	
16	17	18	
23	24	25	
30	31		

August

*Commit to the Lord whatever you do,
and he will establish your plans.*

Proverbs 16:3

Notes

The Lord is my shepherd, I lack nothing.

Psalm 23:1

Reflections

September

Now the Lord is the Spirit, and where the Spirit of the Lord is, there is freedom. — 2 Corinthians 3:17

monday	tuesday	wednesday	thursday
2 Labor Day	3	4	5
9	10	11 Patriot Day	12
16 Stepfamily Day	17 Citizenship Day	18	19
23 30	24	25	26

2024

Lamentations 3:22

*The steadfast love of the Lord never ceases;
his mercies never come to an end.*

friday	saturday	sunday
		1
6	7	8 Grandparents' Day
13	14	15
20	21	22
27	28	29

September

*We are confident, I say, and would prefer to be away
from the body and at home with the Lord.*

2 Corinthians 5:8

Notes

Taste and see that the Lord is good; blessed is the one who takes refuge in him.

Psalm 34:8

Reflections

October

The Lord turn his face toward you and give you peace. Numbers 6:26

monday	tuesday	wednesday	thursday
	1	2	3 Rosh Hashana
7	8	9	10
14 Columbus Day	15	16	17 Sukkot
21	22	23	24
28	29	30	31 Halloween

2024

1 John 3:2 *Now we are children of God, and what we will be has not yet been made known.*

friday	saturday	sunday
4	5	6
11	12 Yom Kippur	13
18	19	20
25	26	27

October

Whatever you ask in prayer, you will receive, if you have faith.

Matthew 21:22

Notes

And we know that in all things God works for the good of those who love him.

Romans 8:28

Reflections

November

*Once you were not a people,
but now you are the people of God.*   1 Peter 2:10

monday	tuesday	wednesday	thursday
4	5	6	7
11 Veterans' Day	12	13	14
18	19	20	21
25	26	27	28 Thanksgiving

2024

Matthew 5:4

*Blessed are those who mourn,
for they will be comforted.*

friday	saturday	sunday
1	2	3 Daylight Saving Ends
8	9	10
15	16	17
22	23	24
29 Black Friday	30	

November

Cast all your anxiety on him because he cares for you.

1 Peter 5:7

Notes

You are the God who performs miracles;
you display your power among the peoples.

Psalm 77:14

Reflections

December

Be careful not to practice your righteousness in front of others to be seen by them. — Matthew 6:1

monday	tuesday	wednesday	thursday
2 Cyber Monday	3	4	5
9	10	11	12
16	17	18	19
23	24 Christmas Eve	25 Christmas Day	26 Hanukkah
30	31 New Year's Eve		

2024

The testing of your faith produces steadfastness.

James 1:3

friday	saturday	sunday	
		1	
6	7 Pearl Harbor Remembrance Day	8	
13	14	15	
20	21	22	
27	28	29	

December

*There is surely a future hope for you,
and your hope will not be cut off.*

Proverbs 23:18

Notes

Do not let your hearts be troubled and do not be afraid.

John 14:27

Reflections

My 2025 Resolutions

1
2
3
4
5
6
7
8
9
10
11
12
13
14
15
16
17
18

May he give you the desire of your heart and make all your plans succeed.

— Psalm 20:4

January

The name of the Lord is a strong tower;
The righteous run to it and are safe.   Proverbs 18:10

monday	tuesday	wednesday	thursday
		1 New Year's Day	2
6	7	8	9
13	14	15	16
20 Martin Luther King Day	21	22	23
27	28	29	30

2025

Psalm 18:32

God arms me with strength, and he makes my way perfect.

friday	saturday	sunday
3	4	5
10	11	12
17	18	19
24	25	26
31		

January

*God's love has been poured out into our hearts
through the Holy Spirit, who has been given to us.*

Romans 5:5

Notes

I can do all this through him who gives me strength.

Philippians 4:13

Reflections

February

Blessed is the one who trusts in the Lord, whose confidence is in him. — Jeremiah 17:7

monday	tuesday	wednesday	thursday
3	4	5	6
10	11	12	13
17 Presidents Day	18	19	20
24	25	26	27

2025

Psalm 107:1

*Give thanks to the Lord, for he is good;
his love endures forever.*

friday	saturday	sunday
	1	2 Groundhog Day
7	8	9
14 Valentine's Day	15	16
21	22	23
28		

February

The Lord is my rock, my fortress and my deliverer.

Psalms 18:2

Notes

2025

I am the resurrection and the life; the one who believes in me will live, even though they die.

John 11:25

Reflections

March

Whoever pursues righteousness and love finds life, prosperity and honor. Proverbs 21:21

monday	tuesday	wednesday	thursday
3	4 Mardi Gras	5	6
10	11	12	13
17 St. Patrick's Day	18	19	20
24	25	26	27
31 Eid al-Fitr			

2025

Hebrews 10:22

Let us draw near to God with a sincere heart and with the full assurance that faith brings.

friday	saturday	sunday
	1	2
	Ramadan	
7	8	9
		Daylight Saving Starts
14	15	16
Purim		
21	22	23
28	29	30

March

*Consider it pure joy, my brothers and sisters,
whenever you face trials of many kinds.*

James 1:2

Notes

Be joyful in hope, patient in affliction, faithful in prayer.

Romans 12:12

Reflections

April

*God is our refuge and strength,
an ever-present help in trouble.*   Psalms 46:1

monday	tuesday	wednesday	thursday
	1 April Fool's Day	2	3
7	8	9	10
14	15	16	17
21	22 Earth Day	23	24
28	29	30	

2025

Colossians 1:17 — *He is before all things, and in Him all things hold together.*

friday	saturday	sunday
4	5	6
11	12	13 Passover
18 Good Friday	19	20 Easter
25	26	27

April

*That your faith might not rest in the wisdom
of men but in the power of God.*

1 Corinthians 2:5

Notes

A friend loves at all times.

Proverbs 17:17

Reflections

May

Be on your guard, stand firm in the faith, be courageous, be strong. — 1 Corinthians 16:13

monday	tuesday	wednesday	thursday
			1
5 Cinco de Mayo	6	7	8
12	13	14	15
19	20	21	22
26 Memorial Day	27	28	29

2025

Be kind and compassionate to one another, forgiving each other, just as in Christ God forgave you.
Ephesians 4:32

friday	saturday	sunday
2	3	4
9	10	11 Mother's Day
16	17 Armed Forces Day	18
23	24	25
30	31	

May

The world and its desires pass away, but whoever does the will of God lives forever.

1 John 2:17

Notes

*Come to me, all you who are weary and burdened,
and I will give you rest.*

Matthew 11:28

Reflections

June

The Lord is my strength and my song; he has given me victory.   *Psalm 118:14*

monday	tuesday	wednesday	thursday
2	3	4	5
Shavuot			
9	10	11	12
16	17	18	19
23	24	25	26
30			

2025

Philippians 4:6

Do not be anxious about anything, but in every situation, by prayer and petition, with thanksgiving, present your requests to God.

friday	saturday	sunday
		1
6	7	8
	Eid al-Adha	Pentecost
13	14	15
	Flag Day	Father's Day
20	21	22
27	28	29
Muharram		

June

*The Lord, the Lord himself, is my strength and my defense,
he has become my salvation.*

Isaiah 12:2

Notes

Whatever you do, work at it with all your heart, as working for the Lord.

Colossians 3:23

Reflections

July

*In this world you will have trouble.
But take heart! I have overcome the world.*   John 16:33

monday	tuesday	wednesday	thursday
	1	2	3
7	8	9	10
14 Bastille Day	15	16	17
21	22	23	24
28	29	30	31

2025

1 Thessalonians 5:11

Encourage one another and build each other up, just as in fact you are doing.

friday	saturday	sunday
4	5	6
11	12	13
18	19	20
25	26	27 Parents' Day

July

*Search for the Lord and for his strength;
continually seek him.*

1 Chronicles 16:11

Notes

*The Lord will watch over your coming
and going both now and forevermore.*

Psalms 121:8

Reflections

August

The Lord will indeed give what is good, and our land will yield its harvest.   Psalm 85:11-13

monday	tuesday	wednesday	thursday
4	5	6	7
11	12	13	14
18	19	20	21
25	26	27	28

2025

Romans 12:8

If it is to encourage, then give encouragement; if it is giving, then give generously; if it is to lead, do it diligently; if it is to show mercy, do it cheerfully.

friday	saturday	sunday
1	2	3
8	9	10
15	16	17
22	23	24
29	30	31

August

*May the God of hope fill you with all joy
and peace as you trust in him.*

Romans 15:13

Notes

When I am afraid, I put my trust in You.

Psalm 56:3

Reflections

September

He gives strength to the weary and increases the power of the weak. — Isaiah 40:29

monday	tuesday	wednesday	thursday
1 Labor Day	2	3	4
8	9	10	11 Patriot Day
15	16 Stepfamily Day	17 Citizenship Day	18
22	23 Rosh Hashana	24	25
29	30		

2025

Psalm 143:8

Let the morning bring me word of Your unfailing love, for I have put my trust in You.

friday	saturday	sunday
5	6	7 Grandparents' Day
12	13	14
19	20	21
26	27	28

September

This is the confidence we have in approaching God: that if we ask anything according to his will, he hears us.

1 John 5:14

Notes

My flesh and my heart may fail, but God is the strength of my heart and my portion forever.

Psalm 73:26

Reflections

October

Let us be sober, putting on faith and love as a breastplate, and the hope of salvation as a helmet. — *1 Thessalonians 5:8*

monday	tuesday	wednesday	thursday
		1	2 Yom Kippur
6	7	8	9
	Sukkot		
13 Columbus Day	14	15	16
20	21	22	23
27	28	29	30

The Lord your God will be with you wherever you go.
Joshua 1:9

2025

friday	saturday	sunday
3	4	5
10	11	12
17	18	19
24	25	26
31 Halloween		

October

The righteous will live by faith.

Romans 1:17

Notes

For the Spirit God gave us does not make us timid, but gives us power, love and self-discipline.

2 Timothy 1:7

Reflections

November

So in Christ Jesus you are all children of God through faith.   Galatians 3:26

monday	tuesday	wednesday	thursday
3	4	5	6
10	11 *Veterans' Day*	12	13
17	18	19	20
24	25	26	27 Thanksgiving

2025

For we walk by faith, not by sight.
2 Corinthians 5:7

friday	saturday	sunday
	1	2 Daylight Saving Ends
7	8	9
14	15	16
21	22	23
28 Black Friday	29	30

November

Rejoice always, pray continually, give thanks in all circumstances; for this is God's will for you in Christ Jesus.

1 Thessalonians 5:16-18

Notes

Be strong and take heart, all you who hope in the Lord.

Psalms 31:24

Reflections

December

He gives showers of rain to all people, and plants of the field to everyone. *Zechariah 10:1*

monday	tuesday	wednesday	thursday
1 Cyber Monday	2	3	4
8	9	10	11
15 Hanukkah	16	17	18
22	23	24 Christmas Eve	25 Christmas Day
29	30	31 New Year's Eve	

2025

*Greater love has no one than this:
to lay down one's life for one's friends.*

John 15:13

friday	saturday	sunday
5	6	7 Pearl Harbor Remembrance Day
12	13	14
19	20	21
26	27	28

December

You are the God who performs miracles;
you display your power among the peoples.

Psalm 77:14

Notes

The Lord will do what is good in his sight.

2 Samuel 10:12

Reflections

www.ingramcontent.com/pod-product-compliance
Lightning Source LLC
LaVergne TN
LVHW020425070526
838199LV00003B/279